Charlie's Best Work Yet

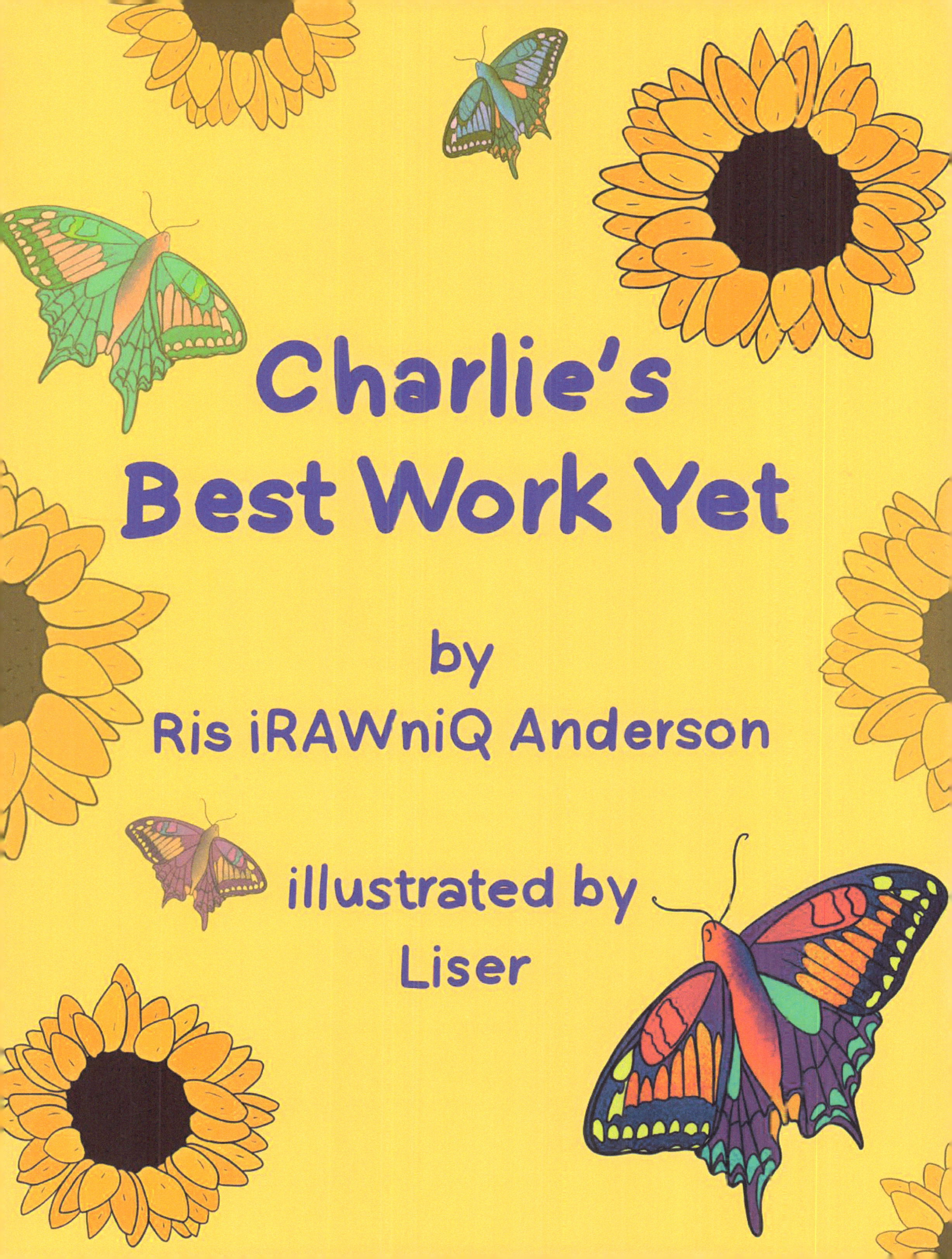

Charlie's Best Work Yet

by
Ris iRAWniQ Anderson

illustrated by
Liser

CHARLIE'S BEST WORK YET
Copyright © 2020 by Charlie Girl Publishing, LLC

All rights reserved. No part of this book may be reproduced in any form or by any electronic or mechanical means, including information storage and retrieval systems, without permission in writing from the publisher, except by a reviewer who may quote brief passages in a review.

This is a work of fiction. Names, characters, places, and incidents either are the product of the author's imagination or are used fictitiously. Any resemblance to actual persons, living or dead, events, or locales is entirely coincidental.

Illustrations copyright © 2020 by Liser

ISBN 9780578813677 (paper back)
ISBN 9781087930824 (ebook)

To My Dearest Frankie,
thank you for seeing and
accepting the 'real' me.
#RAWandFRANKIE

Charlie was no ordinary 5th grader. She had amazing fashion sense, was an impeccable painter, and loved it when her grandma cooked her breakfast for dinner. She was an androgynous girl and took pride in wearing anything that looked rad.

One sunny afternoon, as she was preparing to leave school for the day, she noticed a flyer posted by her locker. "Talent Show, grand prize $100"! But she doubted she could win.

Just then, the star basketball player Devin walked by and noticed Charlie looking at the flyer.

"Hey, I'm Devin. We catch the same bus, but you're always drawing so you probably never notice. I've seen your drawings and they're fantastic— you should definitely enter the talent show."

Charlie still had doubts, but Devin's compliment gave her courage. She filled out an entry form and wrote "artist" as her talent. She was nervous as she was excited. The two walked together.

"Good afternoon Charlie!" greeted Ms. Bobbi, the bus driver.

"Good afternoon Ms. Bobbi!"

"I love your attire! Looking quite fashionable as always."

Charlie flashed a smile. "Thank you, Ms. Bobbi."

Charlie found an empty seat on the bus and pulled out her drawing pad.

Charlie was an impressive artist. She could hear colors and visualize sound. Art was her FUN place and she truly got lost in it. Her grandma, one of her biggest supporters, would buy Charlie all the art supplies she asked for. But Charlie's thoughts were soon interrupted by a crude voice.

"Well, if it isn't the weirdo, Chuck. What's up, Chuck? What kind of weird stuff are you scribbling in your little diary today?"

It was Ronnie. The biggest, meanest, rudest 5th grader at Starshine Elementary school.

Charlie ignored him and continued to draw.

"Didn't you hear me talking to you, freak? Or are you as confused as you look?"

Some of the kids began to laugh at Charlie.

"Leave her alone, Ronnie!" Can't you find someone your size to pick on?" retorted Devin. "I'm sure you can find a 6th grader to bully. After all, aren't you supposed to be in OUR grade?"

Ronnie narrowed his eyes and retreated. Apparently, he had failed first grade, and this was why he was the biggest 5th grader around.

"Thanks for sticking up for me," Charlie said, embarrassed.

"Most of the time I ignore Ronnie, but sometimes he really hurts my feelings."

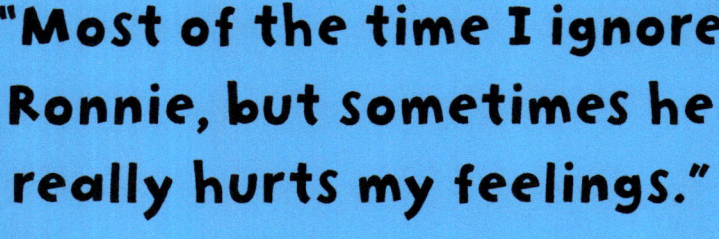

"Hey, no sweat. Jerks like Ronnie prey on kids like us."

"Like us?" asked Charlie.

"Sure. You know, different. We dress differently. Think differently. It's just who we are. By the way, I absolutely love what you're drawing there," Devin said, pointing to Charlie's art.

Charlie froze. She rarely showed her art book to anyone and Devin's excitement embarrassed her.

"I'm into art too! WE are the artists in the world! All the great artists in the world are different! That's what makes them stand out. Here, let me show you something."

Devin reached into her backpack and pulled out a picture of a tall, brown model with short hair.

"This is the iconic Grace Jones!"

"Grace Jones? Who's Grace Jones?"

Devin's eyes became as wide as her smile. "Grace Jones is a supermodel, singer and actress extraordinaire. She's pretty much everything!"

Charlie studied the picture. THIS lady is a supermodel? She thought to herself. She sure didn't look like a supermodel.

Devin must have felt Charlie's skepticism because she continued.

"Grace Jones is one of the most iconic artists ever. I mean, look at her style. Her hair. Her awesomeness! She wears whatever she wants! Her hair is chopped off like a boy's but she doesn't care because she is living her truth."

"That's funny. My grandma always says that we should all live our own truth."

"Well, she's right. Grace Jones is a real artist and doesn't try to fit in. Because real artists never fit in. I carry her picture with me as a reminder to never fit in. She's my inspiration."

Charlie studied the picture of Grace Jones a few seconds longer. Grace was elegant with deep brown silky skin. And she looked very boyish. She looked like nothing in the magazines Grandma had in her office. Charlie was astounded, but more importantly, she was inspired to create.

Devin smiled. "You know what kid, how about you keep this picture? I have tons of Grace's pictures. Consider it a gift— from one artist to another."

When Charlie arrived home, she gathered her art supplies and ran straight to her room. She set up her easel, lined up all of her paints, and pinned the picture of Grace to her pegboard.

Grace had a deep regal complexion. Charlie combined browns and purples and reds until she made *just* the right color. Her hands took over and swayed across the portrait.

Every day after school, Charlie would race straight home and work on her painting. She worked relentlessly until grandma made her stop for dinner.

"Whatever you're drawing, I'm sure it's fantastic," her grandma said with a smile. "But you still need to eat!"

"Grandma, can I have French toast for dinner tonight," Charlie asked.

"I thought you might have a taste for that," Grandma smirked. To Charlie's surprise, Grandma had already cooked her famous strawberry French toast.

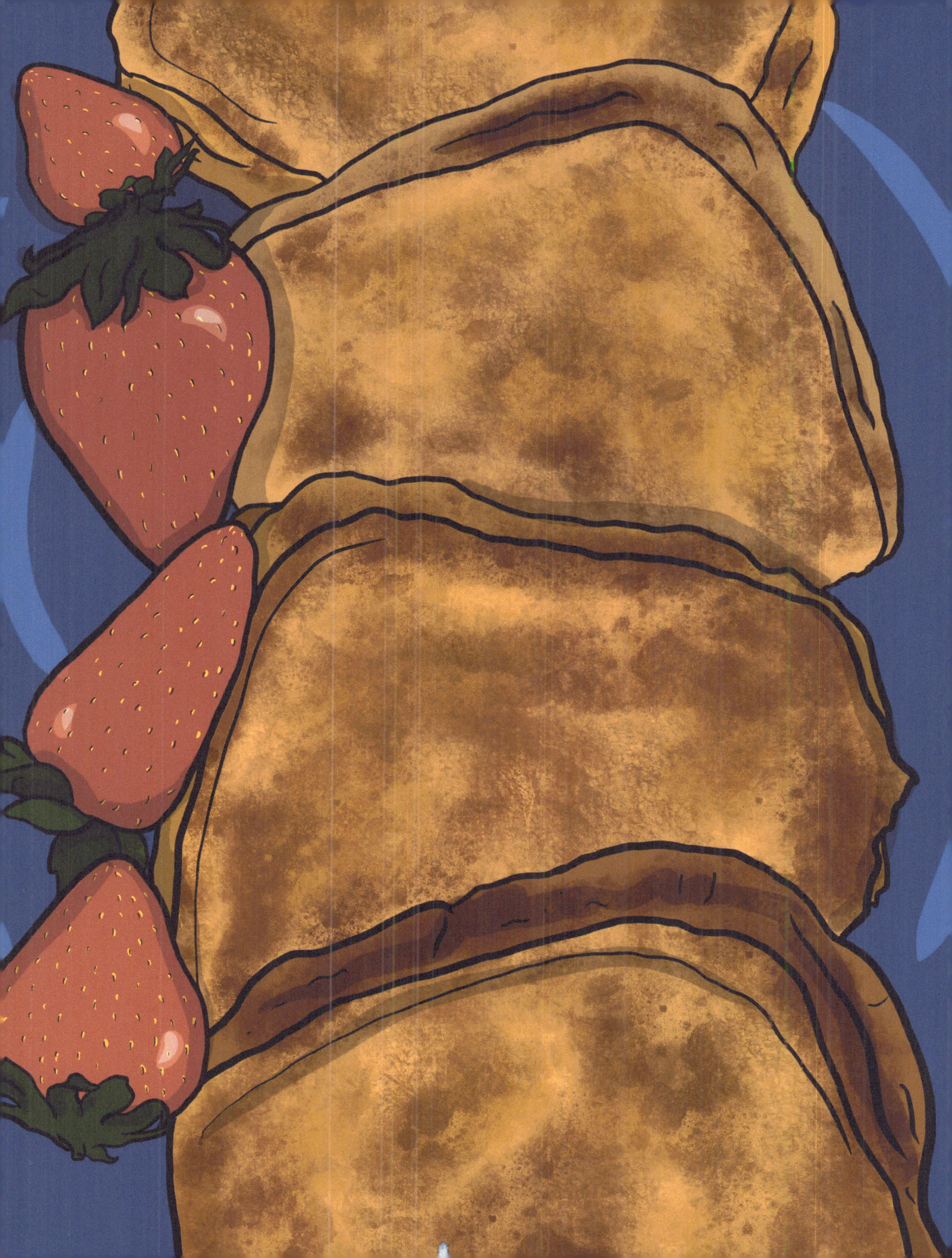

Charlie devoured the French toast in a matter of minutes. She loved how unconventional Grandma was. Grandma *empowered* Charlie and always encouraged her to be unique. She often let Charlie eat breakfast for dinner and encouraged her to dress as she pleased.

One morning on the way to school, Charlie was sketching in her pad like normal and was interrupted by a cacophony of chants.

"Chuck Chuck...Chuck the freak. Chuck the freak and Chuck the geek."

It grew louder.

"Chuck Chuck...Chuck the freak. Chuck the freak and Chuck the geek!"

It was no one else but Ronnie and his crew of scumbags, as Devin once referred to them.

She continued to draw. She dreamed about returning home and adding the finishing touches to her painting. She focused all of her energy into her thoughts, drowning out all of the negative chants. Unable to get a reaction, Ronnie and his crew retreated.

Charlie daydreamed and drew the entire way home and before she knew it, she was nearly at her stop. As she prepared to exit the bus, Ms. Bobbi flashed her a huge smile.

"I knew you wouldn't let those boys get to you, sweetheart," Ms. Bobbi said. "You're something extraordinary. You're a light shining brighter than the brightest star. Remember, it's the moths who are attracted to light!"

Charlie jumped off the bus and raced as quickly as she could to her house. The only thing she had on her mind was her acrylics, her easel, and her painting.

She flung open the front door, threw her belongings on the chair, and raced up the stairs.

Charlie entered her room, threw on her artist apron and began to work.

Charlie combined browns, reds, oranges and purples.

She fused fuchsias with hues of blues.

She blended colors of cantaloupe with corals.

She splashed salmon with strawberry reds.

She bedazzled…

She sparkled…

And voila!

She was finished. She stepped back and looked at the painting, beaming. The talent show was tomorrow, and she was proud.

The night of the talent show made Charlie very anxious. All of the contestants were uber talented. Some sang, danced, and even performed *spoken word*. When it was her turn to present, she carefully held her painting against her chest and slowly walked to the podium.

"My name is Charlie," she said, as her voice trembled like leaves on a branch's edge. "I've been called a weirdo because my hair is cut short. I've been called a freak because I don't play with Barbies or do other girly things. I don't eat meat because animals are my friends. I like to draw and I love to paint. Lots of people make me feel different, but there is one person who never makes me feel like I'm weird, and always helps me
feel good about being me.
I painted that person."

Charlie carefully unwrapped her painting and set it on the easel. The lights from the stage reflected off the painting, illuminating the picture like never before! The colors were so sensational you could almost taste them. Students and parents began to cheer. "I present to you: my grandma!"

"That's sooo rad!" yelled someone from the audience.

Charlie was overwhelmed with happiness. She had not been expecting it. It made her feel like a true artist.

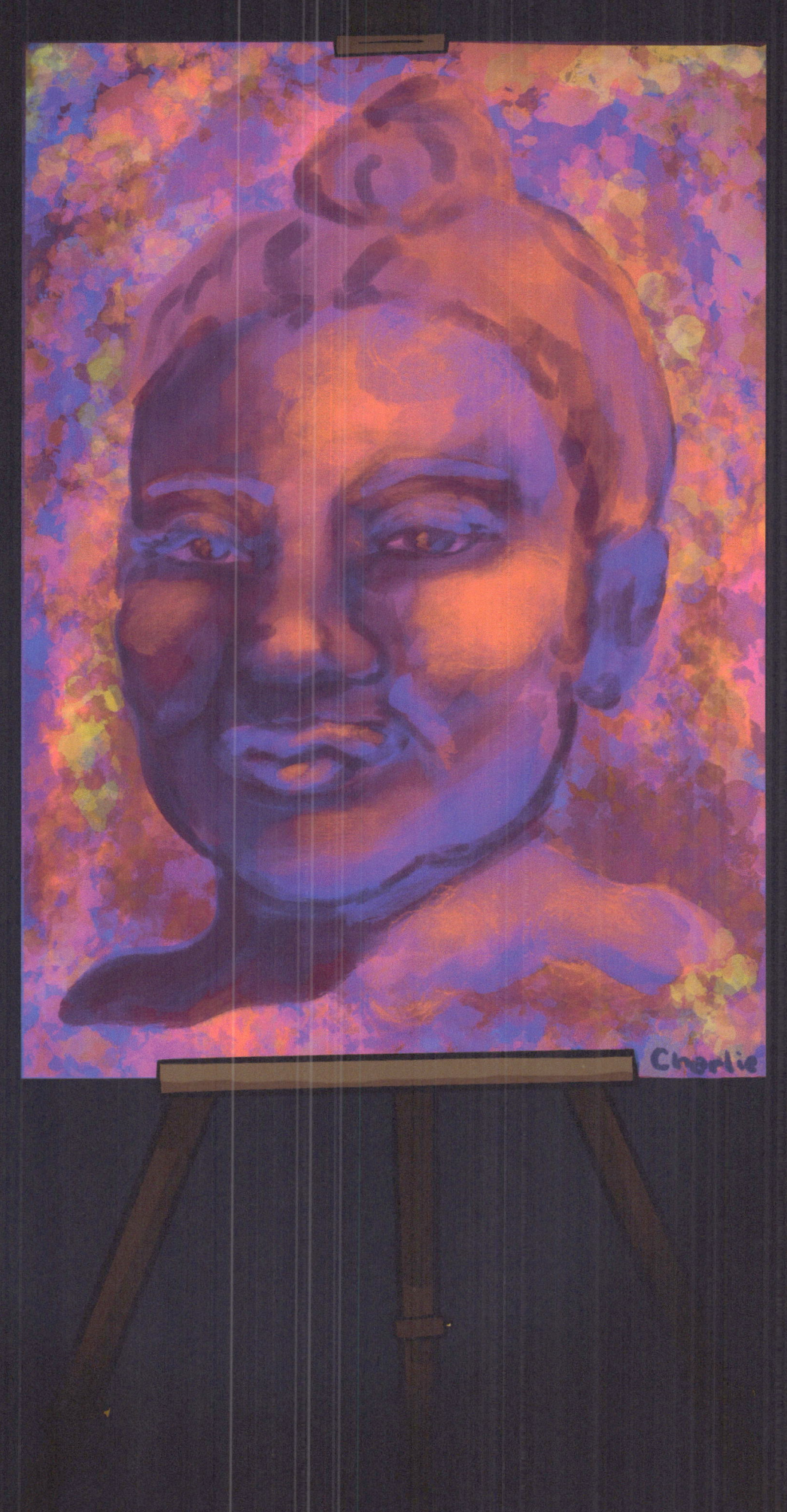

Later that night, the winner of the contest was announced. But it was not Charlie. She didn't cry, she didn't sulk. She was proud of herself and her painting. It was true she didn't win the contest, but she won something greater. She won the right to be herself before the world. What was more? She was inspired. And it felt amazing.

CHARLIE'S VOCABULARY WORDS

Acrylics:

fast drying, water-soluble, paint

Androgynous:

having masculine and feminine characteristics

Cacophony:

a harsh mix of sounds

Empowered:

to give the power to do something

Elegant:

graceful and stylish in appearance or manner

Fused:

joined or blended together

Fuchsias:

a vivid purplish-red color

Iconic:

someone who you want to spend time with and go on any adventure with

Impeccable:

flawless

Regal:

fit for a king or queen, especially in being magnificent or dignified

...you are brilliant.

CPSIA information can be obtained
at www.ICGtesting.com
Printed in the USA
BVHW051503220421
605631BV00002B/174